Mountain bluebirds are eternal optimists. They return from the south in early March, and nearly always have to make it through more than one blizzard before spring really stays warm.

The Beauty of the
BIG HORNS

by Esther McWilliams

(Front cover) *Sunset over the Big Horn Mountains, near Sheridan*
(Back cover) *Flower garden in the wild — mostly lupine and paintbrush*

Published by
Beautiful America Publishing Company
2600 Progress Way
Woodburn, Oregon 97071

Design: Bob Mountain

Library of Congress Catalog Number 98-22671
ISBN 0-89802-699-7

Printed in Korea

BIGHORN FOREST RESERVE

By Executive Order of FEBRUARY 22, 1897, President Grover Cleveland created the BIGHORN FOREST RESERVE, only the second Reserve in the Nation, following the creation of the Yellowstone Timber Land Reserve six years earlier by President Harrison.

The RESERVE includes most of the northern two-thirds of the Bighorn Mountain Range, starting at the Montana border and extending to the south some 75-100 miles, the length not easy to estimate as the range falls off gradually on both ends. The width from base to base ranges from 30 to 50 miles. On the east lies the expanse of the Great Plains and on the west the arid Bighorn Basin.

Structurally the range consists of a great, broad anticlinal fold, steep upon the flanks, with a granite nucleus. Within the rim rock, granite summits rise irregularly, the highest of these being Cloud Peak at 13,175 feet above sea level.

Its surface is drained on the west side by branches of the Bighorn River, on the north by the Little Bighorn, on the north and east by branches of the Tongue River, and on the southeast by the upper forks of the Powder.

— from the 1897-98 Annual Report of the U.S. Geological Survey to the Sec. of Interior

The Act of March 8, 1891 — Creation and Administration of Forest Reserves — allowed the President of the United States to set apart and reserve, in any state or territory, any part of the public lands covered with timber or undergrowth, as public reservations.

The forest reserves were established to improve and protect the forest within the reserve, for the purpose of securing favorable conditions of water flows, and to furnish a continuous supply of timber for the use and necessities of the citizens of the United States.

Congress took this action because the forests of the great mountain ranges in the West were being destroyed very rapidly by fire and reckless cutting. It was realized that unless something was done to protect them, the timber resources of the country and the many industries dependent upon the forest would be badly crippled. The law aimed to save the timber for the use of the people and to hold the mountain forests as great sponges to give out steady flows of water for use in the fertile valleys below.

At the start, there was much opposition to the forest reserves. Often this opposition was just; for although Congress had set aside the lands and their resources, it had made little provision for their administration and protection, which was both ineffectual and annoying to local interests. The timber was simply locked up and allowed to burn. The situation was remedied with the Organic Administration Act of June 4, 1897, and several subsequent amendments, which made it possible to use all the resources and give them suitable protection.

The Transfer Act of February 1, 1905, transferred jurisdiction over the forest reserves to the Secretary of Agriculture, renaming them national forests, and creating the United States Forest Service. The implementing policy for that Act by the Secretary of Agriculture, and the first chief forester, Gifford Pinchot, in part states:

All land is to be devoted to its most productive use for the permanent good of the whole people, and not for the temporary benefit of individuals or companies. All the resources of National Forests are for use, in a thoroughly prompt and businesslike manner, under such restrictions only as will ensure the permanence of these resources.

The wood, water, and forage of the reserves are to be conserved and wisely used for the benefit of the home builder . . . and continued prosperity of the agricultural, lumbering, mining, and livestock interests who are dependent upon a permanent and accessible supply of water, wood, and forage.

Where conflicting interests must be reconciled, the question will always be decided from the standpoint of the <u>greatest good of the greatest number in the long run.</u>

— Regulations & Instructions for the Use of the National Forest Reserves USDA, Forest Service, July 1, 1906

CONTRIBUTORS

I wish to thank the following people for their <u>very</u> generous financial contributions to this book. My heartfelt "Thanks!" go out to all of you, for without <u>your</u> efforts, its printing would not have been possible:

Bighorn Mountain Country Coalition

The MARY ALICE FORTIN FOUNDATION, Inc., in dedication to Cal and Irene Taggart of Lovell, Wyoming

Pepsi-Cola Bottlers of Wyoming, based in Worland, Wyoming

The NEWELL B. SARGENT FOUNDATION (Newell and Vera Sargent) of Worland, Wyoming

Shoshone Distributing Company of Cody, Wyoming

The Rural Development and Community Assistance programs available through the United States Forest Service

ACKNOWLEDGMENTS

While all of the photographs in this book are mine that I have taken over a period of many years, and the captions and a portion of the text are as well, I want to gratefully acknowledge the contributions of a number of other people in helping make this book about my Beautiful Bighorns possible:

— The historical accounts and natural resource information were researched and prepared by Robert E. Mountain, USDA Forest Service.
— I especially appreciate the advice and assistance of Mike Johnson of Shoshone Distributing in Cody—and thank him for his generous donation.
— To BigHorn Mountain Country Coalition Executive Director Donald L. McCracken, Jr. For his final review and his efforts to secure funding for the book.
— The Bighorn Sheep tracks are adapted from those shown in *The Peterson Field Guide Series: A Field Guide to Animal Tracks,* by Olaus J. Murie.
— The figures of the Bighorn Sheep used throughout the book are from a drawing courtesy of Connie Robinson.

DEDICATION

Many people have helped me over the years, and encouraged me to share my Big Horn "treasures" with the rest of the world. I dedicate this book to Mary & Bob and Bob & Carol; without them, it would never have happened.

Sunrise on the Big Horns, taken from Jim Creek Hill southeast of Sheridan on Highway 14

There is no way words can express what it means to me to be part owner of over one million acres of some of the most beautiful land on earth — the Bighorn National Forest. For that matter, I am a citizen and therefore part owner of many more millions of acres of public land all over the United States, and all of it is staffed by dedicated, hard-working people who are taking care of it for me.

What incredible riches! I have lived below the poverty line for most of my life, but I have wealth beyond the wildest dreams of the ancient nobility or the financial magnates of modern times. The beauty of my wealth — the public lands — is that it can be shared with all — it belongs to all! Now, and for future generations.

I've never been one to find my renewal in man-made churches. I have to get mine at the source. No matter how frazzled or blue I may be, a day of basking in the glory of my mountains lifts me up, sets me free, gives me a sense of balance that I sorely need. Whether it is a spectacular vista from a high place, a crashing weather show, a soft dreamy time by a tiny brook tinkling through the flowers, this is where I find food for my soul.

In all the universe, there are no jewels more lovely than dewdrops on a flower petal. The water gathers in the crystal streams, and sings a wild little song as it plunges boldly on its journey to the sea. There it will rise up again to make the clouds that form the glorious sunrises and sunsets that fill me with reverent awe, and who knows how many generations later the water comes back again to gather on flower petals and twinkle little rainbows at me in the rays of the rising sun. You can keep your diamonds. They can't compare with the "jewels" I already have.

— *Esther*

A jeweled lupine leaf

(Opposite) Sunrise on the Big Horns, again from Jim Creek Hill. The curved mountain on the left is Cloud Peak, and the dark point on the right is Blacktooth; both are within the boundary of the Cloud Peak Wilderness.

Mountain meadows have a way of lifting the heart with their glory. Here we find mostly lupine and wild geranium, near Burgess Junction.

Tensleep Canyon, looking west down Highway 16 toward the Big Horn Basin

Sometimes the Sheridan valley fills up with fog, here seen from a hill near Wolf Creek.

Young mule deer saying "Hi"

Evening light on a rocky point near Sibley Lake

A pristine snowscape on Highway 14

Alpine sunflower, Old-Man-of-the-Mountains — whatever you call it — is a startlingly large flower 2-4 inches across and seldom over a foot tall. All are facing east on alpine meadows. Chickweed is in the background.

Gathering the cattle in upper Shell Canyon east of Greybull; it's time to take them back to the Big Horn Basin for the winter.

Early spring on the North Fork of the Tongue River, from Highway 14

Redtwig dogwood leaves

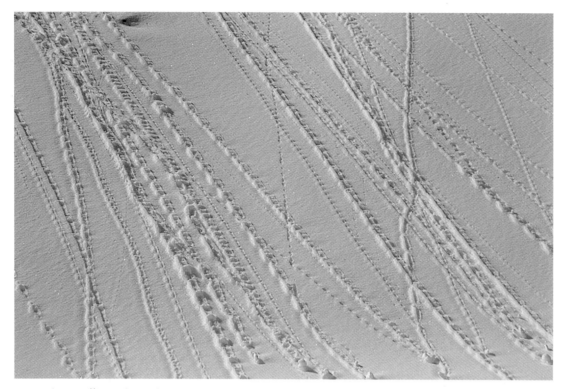

Snow drops off pine branches on a steep hill and makes trail patterns as it tumbles down the slope.

A black-capped chickadee is always a joy — winter or summer.

20

Early spring on the North Fork of the Tongue River, from Highway 14

Redtwig dogwood leaves

Don't let a change in the weather discourage you from a trip to the mountain! Lodgepole pine forest sleeps in a heavy fog.

A spring riot of arrowleaf balsamroot near Steamboat Point west of Dayton

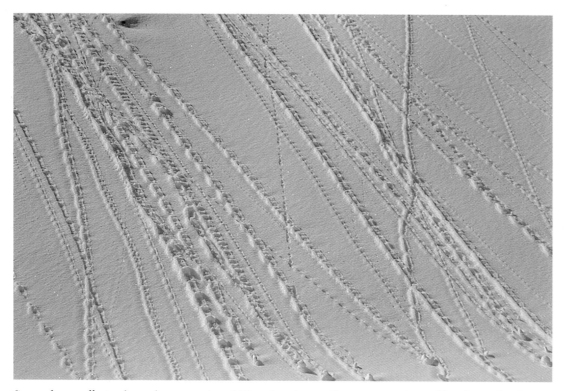

Snow drops off pine branches on a steep hill and makes trail patterns as it tumbles down the slope.

A black-capped chickadee is always a joy — winter or summer.

20

Lake Solitude in the Cloud Peak Wilderness — in late August!

View from Tunnel Hill near Story

Ice fishing on Meadowlark Lake on Highway 16

Striped coralroot, a member of the orchid family

Evidence of the burn in Shell Canyon; the fire alongside Highway 14 was started in July of 1984 by children playing with fireworks.

(Opposite) Ponderosa pine trees in the sun

Sunset — One thing about this country is that the scenery in the sky is as interesting as the land.

Dude ranch horses near Wolf, Wyoming

The west side of the Big Horns is very different from the east side, as shown in the next six scenes. Less rainfall provides the look of a real desert.

"Painted desert" from Highway 16

Overlook at Bighorn Canyon National Recreation Area, northeast of Lovell.

28

Castle Gardens is a majestic eroded area near Highway 16 west of Tensleep, Wyoming

Scene in the Devil's Kitchen, another very different eroded area off Highway 14 west of Shell, Wyoming

Ridge beside the road on Highway 16, west of Tensleep

Bighorn Sheep were absent from their namesake mountains for many years, but were reintroduced in the 1990s in Shell Canyon.

South Tongue River from Sawmill Divide road

*Pack train winds its way up the mountain from Eatons'
Ranch west of Sheridan*

*Tiny rills of water are jewels of beauty in many places in the mountains. Yellow monkeyflowers
grace the edges.*

31

Porcupine Falls, north of Highway 14A, drops just over two hundred feet

You always need to be ready for a weather change.

Aspen grove in early spring

Telesonix makes a career of decorating limestone rocks

Sand Turn on Highway 14 is a good place to watch weather in the Sheridan valley.

A visitor demonstrates what some people feel is the ultimate in recreation.

Shell Falls, with the light just right

(Opposite) Another sunrise spectacular

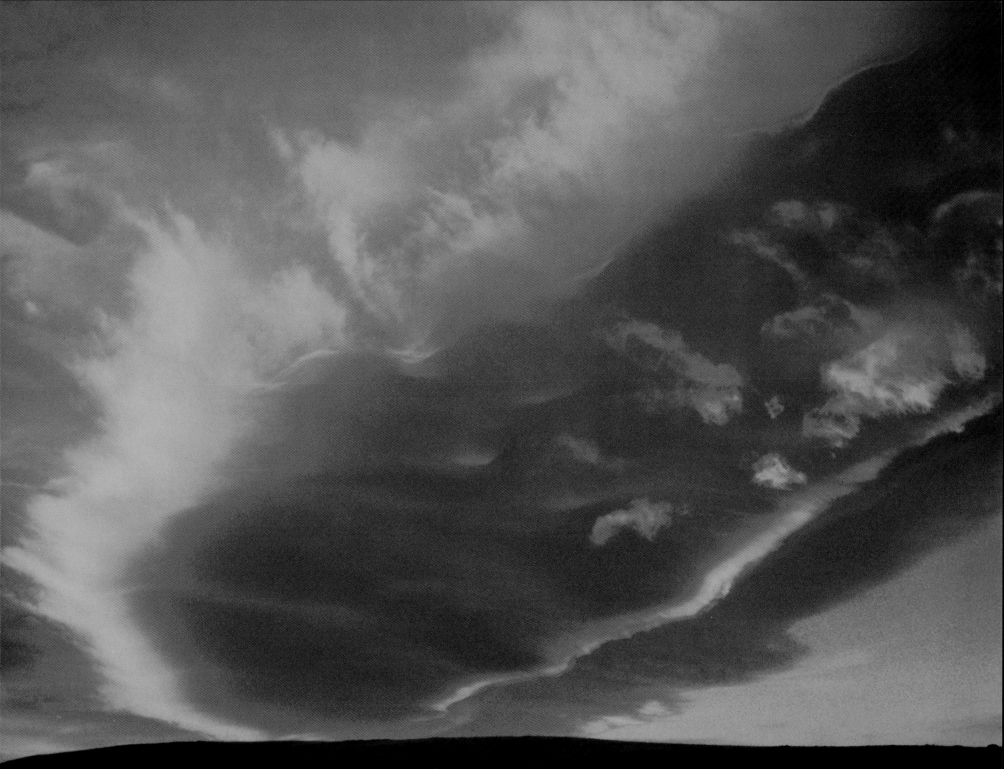

Western tanager

Often it seems little mini-landscapes hold more beauty than vast expanses

Mule deer buck

Winter and early spring have their own warm colors, as seen in this streambed full of willows near Powder River Pass on Highway 16.

(Opposite) *Tongue River Canyon, west of Dayton, dressed in its fall finery*

Getting serious about fun in the outdoors

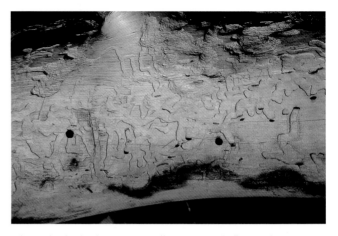

I love the little things; even "worm tracks" on a log can make intriguing patterns.

Crazy Woman Creek, in the canyon, west of Buffalo, Wyoming

42

Would you call this a meadow of lodgepole pine?

43

"Broken heart rock" beside Highway 16, as you start up the mountain west of Buffalo

Sunrise surprise

With its half-and-half mix of timbered areas and open parks, the Bighorns are very well adapted to grazing by sheep.

A century ago, perhaps as many as 450,000 sheep grazed the Forest Reserve. The bands would use the lower foothills in the spring, gradually working upward as the snows melted away, spending the summers in the highest parks. The first snows of early autumn would start them downward once again, in this way securing pasture for about five, occasionally six, months each year.

As the decades have passed, sheep numbers have dwindled to only a fraction of their earlier prominence. Declining demand for wool and meat, economics of the operations, harsh winters, problems with predators, difficulty in locating dependable and willing herders — all have contributed to the reduction of sheep grazing over the years.

As the Forest begins its second century, only about 25,000 sheep are permitted to graze the higher elevations, and the climate has shown over time that a use season of only three to four months is consistently practical in the Bighorns.

Sheep on Hunt Mountain on Highway 14A

Spring runoff in Wolf Creek

Spring is really here when the pasqueflower blooms.

Lichen on an old stump

Whitetail fawn

From the beginning of time, lightning strikes have been a natural part of the landscape, and the resulting wildfires have been a normal, expected occurrence. However, as the nation was settled over a period of some three hundred years, an awareness of the danger from and loss of timber to wildfires caused people to start changing the natural order of things.

The 1897 Report by the Geological Survey speaks of "the destruction of these forests by repeated fires" and "extensive areas in the Reserve which have been devastated by fires of more or less recent date."

Throughout most of the last 100 years, the U.S. Forest Service and other agencies have tried to eliminate the "evil" of fire from forested lands. The belief that all fires were harmful and should be immediately snuffed out had become extremely popular — and prevalent.

The Bighorn usually has less than two dozen small fires each year, and many of these are caused by man. On the average, the forest experiences only two or three fires each decade that may reach a few thousand acres in size.

Extensive research now shows that the exclusion of fire from the ecosystem is creating unhealthy, overcrowded forests that contain more fuel for larger, more severe fires. These larger, intense fires often result in greater impact to soil, water, and air — and, sometimes, to the private homes and property that adjoin the forests — than a managed, prescribed fire.

In many cases, the individual trees have been protected for years, but at the expense of the larger forest community.

As the American public, and forest managers, understand that fire is a natural and revitalizing process, they must also accept that fire's return to the landscape is not without some degree of risk. There will be hazy skies, and patches of blackened forests for a while, and there is always a chance of a fire becoming too large.

The reality is that fire is essential to renew the landscape and stimulate new life. And after a hundred years of control, fire is once again resuming more of the role that nature intended.

Fireweed blooming in a burned-over area, three years after the 1988 Intermission Fire near Bald Mountain on Highway 14A.

Aspen grove near Highway 14, heading down Shell Canyon

Birds in the Bighorn National Forest are variable in size, from this wee ruby-crowned kinglet . . .

. . . to the stately sandhill crane. Both of them nest here.

Another sunrise — how gaudy can you get?

Wolf Creek, west of Sheridan

A creeklet being put to its best use

Cloud Peak and its
cirques from the air

Spring is a fickle spirit . . .

. . . fall is, too! Snow often comes when the leaves are still green.

56

Lake Sibley, beside Highway 14

Moosefest in a meadow near Sawmill Divide

The wilderness high country from the west, at the Freezeout overlook

I'm indulging in my joy of the beauty of "little things."

The thing is, even the same rock is never the same twice. Here are four views of Steamboat Point, the latter from the vantage point of Black Mountain Lookout . . .

Blacktooth Mountain in various
moods. I never use filters.
The sunset version is for REAL!

When I hear about refugees — from whatever cause — pining for their homeland, I get a big lump of empathy in my throat. I left my homeland for a few years, but I managed to return. Whenever I visited during those times, when my beautiful Big Horns came into view, I choked up so I had to pull over and mop my eyes back into driving condition.

I wish to send a sympathy card to those who hesitate for two minutes by the roadside to take a quick look, and then move on. "Ya seen one pile of mountains, ya seen 'em all." They miss so much.

The world abounds in beautiful places: deserts, jungles, seacoasts, tidy farmlands — all are lovely in their own ways. Alps, Himalayas, Andes — their spectacular beauty is a gift to us all over the world. Wildflowers can gladden the heart even in a waste area at the edge of a city lot.

What I am trying to do here is take a *closer* look — a long, loving look — at my home place to show not only what I find glorious in it, but to express how people feel wherever they live when they take their homelands into their hearts, and *cherish* that place.

—Esther

Big Horns in early spring, taken from Moore's Slough near Lake DeSmet, between Buffalo and Sheridan.

The original travel route over the Big Horns—legends telling of a "crazy woman" living along the creek may have been the source of the area's modern-day name. The road now, as then, is not designed for use by low-clearance passenger cars, especially during periods of inclement weather!

Southwest of Buffalo, looking up Crazy Woman Canyon

Crazy Woman Canyon, looking down

Wonderfully jagged spires at the mouth of Crazy Woman Canyon

View from Billy Creek Road, near the Hazelton Road on Highway 16

Elk yearling on a foggy winter day

(Opposite) "Hole-in-the-Wall" country near Kaycee

Western meadowlark — the Wyoming state bird

"Campin' out"

Sego lily

Indian paintbrush (the Wyoming state flower) has a wide range of colors, all these plus blends and pure white and yellow. Wyoming has 20-some species, and some of these hybridize.

I make it a point to never try to key a Castilleja!

A baby antelope

The "Keyhole" in Tongue River Canyon west of Dayton and Ranchester

Two views of Shell Canyon

Call it prairie smoke, old man's whiskers, three-flowered avens, cowboy rose — choose your favorite name.

Shell Creek

Some of my favorite "little things" are the beautiful "gems" of ice along mountain streams . . .

Near Burgess Junction — mostly wild geranium

Elgin Park Loop, from Highway 16 — mostly lupine

Medicine Mountain road — mostly phlox

The thing about mountain meadows
is that no two are alike, they are
never the same for two weeks at a
time, and they're never the same for
two years in succession.

Alpine meadow on Hunt Mountain — a little of everything

83

Bull elk relaxing

Are you ready for another brilliant sunrise?

Blue grouse

The "heart" in Shell Canyon, near Shell Falls

86

The wonderful messy variety of an old growth forest of Engelmann spruce and subalpine fir

View of Sheridan valley from Red Grade Road

Wildflower garden — lupine, paintbrush, shrubby cinque-foil, with a splash of Siberian chives — makes a brilliant bouquet.

Aspen leaves

Pika — This tiny, rabbit-like animal with the high-pitched "squeak" lives in the rock outcrops at the highest elevations, and, instead of hibernating, cures and stores "hay" to survive the harsh winters.

Rocky rim from Highway 14, south of Burgess Junction

91

Fledgling cedar waxwings

Near Hunter Corrals, west of Buffalo

Snowmobiling on Meadowlark Lake on Highway 16

Shooting star

Telesonix foliage in the fall

(Opposite) My kind of mountain activity

Juniper after a rain

Aspen grove

Serviceberry

Waterbabies

(Opposite) Good timing on a windy morning

Sunrise — each one's different.

Monarch butterfly

Water striders — wildlife doesn't have to be big to be worth watching!

Cottonwoods dressed in spring green

102

Windstorm on the high peaks above Buffalo

We don't have free-roaming buffalo any more, but this old crooked-horn cow at the mouth of Tongue River Canyon evokes the wild old days.

103

This shot of Wolf Canyon in fall is not only a nice splash of color, but it also shows a good example of a geologic fault.

Approximately 3,000 cattle grazed the Reserve at the beginning of the 1900s, with most of these animals owned by cattlemen running small ranches in the Bighorn Basin.

Over the years, increasing cattle herds had gradually replaced many of the bands of sheep, and perhaps as many as 50,000 cattle grazed the Forest during a six-month use season in the 1950s. A century after its creation, the Bighorn still permits nearly 28,000 cattle to graze during the summer months.

Of particular concern for today's cattle ranchers and forest managers is the condition of riparian areas — water-influenced zones around lakes and along creeks and rivers. It is there that grass production is the highest and water is readily available; cattle like to congregate in these areas, seeking the shade, cooler temperatures, and good forage they provide.

Summer grazing in the Big Horns

However, the lush grasses, aspens and cottonwoods, and willows and other shrubs in the riparian areas are also much in demand for use by many of the forest's wildlife species — birds for nesting and raising their young, big game for forage and hiding cover, small mammals and furbearers for their homes, and, of course, fish and other species found in and around water — and that includes fishermen and campers!

The challenge lies in proper use and thoughtful management, with a vision for true multiple use of the forage and cover in riparian areas — annually leaving enough grass to provide overhanging banks for fish habitat, trap any sediment produced with the spring's snowmelt and runoff, allow for increased growth of trees and shrubs, and also provide the comfort and personal serenity of a "babbling brook" for the Forest visitor.

Bitterroot — Montana's state flower

New spring growth on the trees — mostly Douglas-fir

Peaks from Highway 16 at Pole Creek

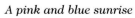

A pink and blue sunrise

A little, wild rock garden

There is no yellow brighter than sunshine through fall aspen leaves.

(Opposite) Winter cloud scene

Llama trekking

Marmots

Invitation to a blissful experience — come on in.

Mountain picnic

Fireweed

112

Whitetail in her bower

Evening light turns the aspens red.

(Opposite) Wolf Creek Canyon

These small, wild bouquets warm the heart.

Hunters on a fall pack trip

South Red Canyon from North Red Canyon, west of Sheridan. These bright red outcrops are familiar sights in the foothills of many Wyoming mountain ranges.

Porcupine

The forest floor

118

One of those chicken-and-egg questions is: do you love a place because you invest a lot of yourself into it, or do you fall in love with the place and then invest yourself? It is an unbroken circle, I think. A place as beautiful as the Big Horn Mountains will capture your heart at first glance, but it is an ongoing wonder to me that the more I glance, look long and deeply, PARTICIPATE in the beauty, the more deeply I love my homeland.

I hope we all will treasure and cherish what we love.

Everything uses the land and ultimately gets its living from the land. Ants use it, birds use it, elk use it, people use it. It is not USING the land that is a bad thing, it is MISUSING it. If whatever is happening now degrades the land so it is diminished for future users, that is misuse.

We have an obligation to see that our ways of making a living do not destroy so much of the land that future people, plants, and other creatures can no longer make a living.

My camera has been my tool for incorporating myself into my homeland. Looking for places and things to photograph concentrates my attention.

The more I look, the more I see. The more intently I see, the more there is to look at. I am frequently surprised by the discovery of wholly new things in places I've been watching intently for many years.

There is no end to the wonder.

—Esther

A sun*set* can be as dramatic as a sun*rise*.

Winter view of Sheridan valley from Sand Point

Mostly lupine, prairie smoke, and cinquefoil

Fallen City, on Highway 14 west of Dayton — a true geologic delight

Aspen leaves in a mountain stream

It is rare to see the pines as wonderfully snow-frosted as they are here.

An all-day picnic ride in Wolf Creek

The 1897 U.S. Geological Survey Report states: "The general aspect of the Bighorn Reserve is that of a lightly forested region. It contains no large or valuable timber. Nearly all has been burned, much of it recently, and a large part has been subjected to repeated fires. A considerable portion of the area consists of open parks. Another large part is covered with a young growth, ranging from 10-50 years of age. As a rule, the trees are small; it is only in limited localities that mature forests exist. And further, the timber which is large enough for use is poor in quality and so full of knots that it could only be used where nothing else was obtainable."

"If this Reserve is treated as a nursery of timber for future use, it becomes a most valuable possession. Only the Federal Government could so hold it as the Trustee for future generations, but so to hold it would be a public benefaction of value which can not now be estimated."

And, indeed, the public has so benefited. Beginning in 1893, timber harvest centered primarily around the production of railroad ties. Tiehack dams and elaborate water flumes were constructed to float the ties off the mountain to the lowlands. The harvesting of timber slowed after 1913. During this period, about 100 million board feet of timber was removed from thousands of acres.

There was a resurgence of commercial logging beginning after World War II due to increased demand for forest products and improved access. The harvest of timber from the Bighorn ranged from five to ten million board feet per year for the next 20 years. Harvest increased dramatically in the 60's, 70's, and 80's, ranging from 10-24 million board feet per year. In the 1990s, due to increasing concerns regarding the effects on other resources, sawtimber harvest decreased to approximately five million board feet per year.

Logging truck, near Burgess Junction

Monkshood

Antelope hang out mostly on the plains around the Big Horns.

High country, as seen from Highway 16.

Prince's pine, or pipsissewa

"Wrinkle Rock" on Highway 14A, on the descent from Bald Mountain to Lovell

Near Powder River Pass

Wild rose

Bucking Mule Falls

Lichen-covered rock, with juniper

Cascading over 500 feet, Bucking Mule Falls and its National Recreation Trail are located in the northwest corner of the Forest, several miles past the Medicine Wheel off Highway 14A.

One more sunrise — we have lots of them!

The road up Medicine Mountain; to the west in the background lies the Bighorn Basin, and the Absaroka Mountains west of Cody are nearly 100 miles in the distance.

The Medicine Wheel from the air

One of the wonder-provoking things about these mountains is finding fossilized coral reefs at 10,000 feet in altitude.

Little Goose Creek, southwest of Sheridan near Big Horn, Wyoming

The Big Horns reflected in a farm pond

A carpet of mountain avens

Fairy slipper, the calypso orchid

Limestone "Castle" on Medicine Mountain

The major tree species found on the Bighorn include lodgepole pine, Engelmann spruce, and subalpine fir; other less-prevalent species include Douglas-fir, ponderosa pine, limber pine, and aspen. The forest ecosystem in the Bighorns is very diverse, ranging from pure stands of even-age lodgepole pine covering thousands of acres to multi-age stands containing a mix of many species. Associated with this forest diversity are many varieties of plants and animals that depend on the forests for their survival.

Forest ecosystems on the Bighorn are constantly changing over time. Sometimes these changes occur very quickly and cover large areas as a result of wildfires or very strong wind storms. For example, in 1993 over two thousand acres of trees blew down as a result of one wind storm and in 1996 approximately four thousand acres were burned in three lightning-caused fires. Events like these — and even larger, though infrequent, ones — are not rare to the Bighorns and are part of the process that creates the variety of ecosystems that make the Forest so interesting and unique.

The forests on the Bighorn, and elsewhere, are important not only for the sustenance of natural systems but also for the use and enjoyment of society. Forest products provided from the Bighorn include sawtimber for manufacture into lumber, house logs, utility poles, posts and poles for fences and corrals, tepee poles, firewood, and Christmas trees.

Current harvest methods on the Forest include several types of partial cutting and occasional clearcutting. The decision of how to best cut timber is complex, and is based on resource objectives such as improving wildlife habitat and diversity and improving

tree growth and health. Factors such as soils, slope, elevation, water, visual quality, and growth and reproductive characteristics of tree species are all taken into account when planning future timber harvests to meet consumer demand.

The decision to harvest trees is complex and often controversial, but forest managers consider it an important tool to accomplish many resource objectives while providing society the wood products it requires. Harvest practices attempt to mimic the patterns and mosaics that nature prescribes through the use of fire and wind.

A regrowing clearcut

From Highway 16, west of Buffalo

The "Pillow Pile" on Sucker Creek, on the Black Mountain Road off Highway 14

Wolf Creek Falls

The "Gargoyles" on Duncum Mountain, north of the Porcupine Ranger Station off Highway 14A

139

Roadcut on Highway 16

Sugarbowl

Antelope Butte Ski Area, between Greybull and Sheridan on Highway 14

Once the railroads penetrated the vast expanses of the West, many of the lands that would later be the National Forests became drawing cards for the people east of the Mississippi. Hot springs, majestic mountain peaks, favorable climates, spectacular vistas—all became areas for those of at least moderate means to visit and enjoy.

In the latter half of the 1900s, with the advent of "easier" lifestyles and increasing amounts of leisure time, recreation became a reality for most Americans, and the focal point for those activities increasingly became the nation's public lands.

Early recreationists tended to participate in "traditional" activities — picnicking, sunbathing, swimming, camping, hiking, hunting, fishing — which were often centered around areas of water, taking place almost entirely in the warm summer months.

At the conclusion of World War II, and the birth of the ski industry, recreation visits increased dramatically, and use of the forests took on a year-round perspective.

As the end of the twentieth century approaches, recreation use continues to skyrocket, and the types of uses are nearly as diverse as the users themselves — jetskiing, snowmobiling, spelunking, rock climbing, hang gliding, mountaineering, helicopter skiing, underwater diving — to name only a few. And the traditional uses of camping, hunting, fishing, and hiking continue to increase significantly as well. The National Forests have truly become America's playgrounds!

The Bighorn has seven resorts and lodges, almost three hundred summer homes, thirty-five campgrounds, two ski areas, over seventy-five miles of groomed cross-country ski trails (another ninety are ungroomed) and almost three hundred miles of groomed snowmobile trails, over a thousand miles and several hundred acres of fishable streams and lakes, hunting opportunities for elk, mule deer, moose, and grouse. Antelope, white-tailed deer, and turkey are found in the lowlands. There are over eleven hundred miles of trails to hike, and all three highways over "the mountain" are designated Scenic Byways.

Opportunities, experiences, vistas, pictures, memories — they abound!

Rocky cliff on Highway 14A

Roadcut of Highway 14   *(Opposite) Aspen grove*

142

The Sheridan valley filled with fog, seen from Sand Point on Highway 14.

purpose and use are as set forth in law. Many people confuse them with National Parks — which are managed for preservation — and that is quite different from the National Forests which are to be managed for conservation and multiple use.

There continues to be misunderstanding and concern and dissatisfaction on the part of many for how their public lands should be managed.

Also remaining is the situation of "opposition to the forest Reserves," although perhaps for different reasons. The concern expressed in 1906 that "the protection of the forest resources still existing is a matter of urgent local and national importance" has proven prophetic indeed.

Increasing numbers of people place greater and greater demands on a resource base that is limited in both size and production capability. As the surrounding private lands have become more developed and increasingly unavailable for public use, people have turned to their National Forests with an expectation that the needs for products, services, qualities, and experiences can yet be met for one and all.

"Many people do not know what National Forests are. Others may have heard much about them, but have no idea of their true purpose and use. A little misunderstanding may cause a great deal of dissatisfaction. The National Forests very closely concern all the people of the West, and, indeed, of the whole country. They affect, directly or indirectly, many great business interests."
— *The Use of the National Forests*
USDA, Gifford Pinchot, Forester
June 14, 1907

Those words of nearly a century ago often ring true today. Many people still do not know what National Forests are — or what their true

The challenge for the second century for the Bighorn National Forest, and all other public lands, may well lie in the ability of the American people and the Forest managers to realize that public lands are no longer able to provide everything for everyone forever.

Only in the attempt to understand the wishes and needs and feelings of others, the ability to give and take in effecting needed compromise, and the desire to truly best manage the land for the generations to come, can "the question always be decided from the standpoint of <u>the greatest good</u> . . .

<u>of the greatest number</u> . . .

<u>in the long run</u>."